SPEAKING PARTS

SPEAKING PARTS

Beth Ruscio

Brick Road Poetry Press
www.brickroadpoetrypress.com

In memory
Kate and Al
who taught me to love the spoken word

Cover art: © 1907, Thomas Anshutz, *A Rose*, at Metropolitan Museum
of Art, New York, NY (www.metmuseum.org)

Author photo: © 2019, Alexis Rhone Fancher

Library of Congress Control Number: 2020932439
ISBN: 978-1-950739-00-4

Published by Brick Road Poetry Press
513 Broadway
Columbus, GA 31902-0751
www.brickroadpoetrypress.com

Brick Road logo by Dwight New

Table of Contents

Subtext

The work is a process of getting lost.
Sometimes you annihilate yourself.

—Dorothea Lange
Grab A Hunk Of Lightning

A Doll's House

To enter she has to get on her hands and knees
to crawl through the front door which naturally
is tight for her. The floors burn her knees.
Once in the front room she can crouch
or when she gets tired of that she can bend over
sideways at the waist enough to clear the ceilings
and of course even lower for the doorways. She bangs
her head on the light fixtures often enough.
Afternoons he likes to have her
serve tea in the tiniest china cups, her fingers
too clumsy for the handles, her thirst
much greater than their capacity.
The clothes he likes her in chafe
and leave marks. He calls her Ducky
the way she waddles in them.
There are no chairs big enough
for her to sit in so she kneels
and when she gets up
which requires his permission
if she winces or even sighs
she prays for a reprimand
because there's worse.

Reclamation

My arms full of washed out
peanut butter jars and other
pampered recyclables,
I'm mistaken for a mother
by the trash man, although
I may also be mistaken
for he is immaculate,
appearing on the running board
of a steamy blue truck on a Friday.
 Happy Mother's Day!
he proclaims buoyantly,
his voice, raspy from talking
over the grind of gears, a dirty job
hauling everyday empties away,
and in return he's joy,
a kind of minister, unsullied.
I don't correct him,
handing over my cans and jars.
I scrubbed them til they gleam
like it's the first day of school.

Correcting for Death

I play this character
   Dead Judith on the call-sheet.
With a paint gun, a makeup specialist in effects
   sprays a dead person's face
   on my face.
Steady, with brushes made of a single eyelash,
   hand mixed color concoctions are applied
   correcting for death.
Stria, for coagulation under the skin.
The mottled freckling of an overripe peach for blood splash.
A sculpted bullet hole in my temple.
An exit wound weeping syrup out my cheek.

Grips remove the rearview mirror
from the 3/4 ton pick-up where I am slaughtered.
   Not for my sake,
   for the camera angle.
I'm in an onion field.
Gore drips off the shattered passenger-side window.
Brains puddle on the Naugahyde seat.

Lunch isn't for hours:
we'll be on this shot forever.

Summary Calling

for John O'Keefe

One season we played nuns, enough to get the feel,
novice actresses yoked to made-up vows,
we bore the marks of wool for weeks,

our skin mercerized in the sunny rehearsal heat—
black gabardine, white challis, black head kerchiefs,
the rubbed-raw badges the costumes chafed

onto our thighs, our wimple-rashed cheeks.
Tested, the long pent-up day of pretend vocation
no lesser devotion, we were cut loose in a red clay field,

the cooling sacrament, dusk,
told to *write loud on a clean red slate*, we formed a kick line,
a cancan in reverse, receding as we curtsied

singing close, a choir of showgirls
charming the fat moon to rise.
We, of the cloth, gone the way of soft rags,

of unanswered rosaries, attended a July reunion,
and up we popped, in unison, as sisters do, forgetting time,
as if strings never untied from habits.

First, we lifted our pretend skirts, our arms akimbo just so,
then without a sideways glance,
set about our magic-seeming backwards trot,

away from our attachments, the trapping world,
our silhouettes scudding like pirate ships
toward the smog rosy light.

Standard Time

There's no saving daylight.
When the sun's too much candy
be glad Fall swallows the days of cherries—
how much Technicolor
can we take? We can't.
Take a load off, dahlias.
Relief. A flatter intonation.
A shorter day. A tonal palette.
Black, grey, white, brown.
A year's implacable yardstick
is in four-four time—
to every thing a turn,
a twelve-bar melody
blooming into call
and response, the soft caress
of Chet Baker's moonlit
What is this thing hooks up
with the percussion of clinking ice
called love? Inevitable.
A blemished plum will rust.
So too a summer crush.
At the season's last happy hour
the night sky, neat, pupils dilated
fervent for its marquee moment—
the long solo. Yes. Raise a glass adieu
to sunburnt days of lemon frazz,
the flushed headiness
at the roller coaster's crest
and the sun too close
for Icarus and the rest.
A swinging back beat, enough
booze and Chinese food
to get us up and running. Rejoice.
This is standard time now, for real.

Counting Off-Whites on the Fingers of One Hand

Alabaster

Halloween is soon, people sizing up their disguises. Like an inside joke, Trash To Treasures Thrift Store holds an annual sale this time of year on used wedding dresses. A large party of empty gowns hangs, deflated, in an October picture window, not one among them what I'd call a *pure white*.

Cream

It's my Tuesday custom to walk by that place on the way to the farmer's market. I am soothed by seasonal turnover—silhouette portraits on sale at Groundhog's Day; next up, Valentine boxer shorts; strawberries before rhubarb before figs. I know tests for best—the freckliest, teen-fuzziest peaches have secret sugar, the lowliest apricots about to turn to mush produce brandy approaching the finest cognac.

Bone

It runs in my family, the love of the shabby genteel, the fostering of underdogs. I married wearing a broken-in vintage frock. Saved, ironed into a precise rectangle, and tucked between layers of acid-free tissue— the second-hand floor length gown with train that my sisters saw me try on and burst into tears: handkerchief cotton batiste, mother-of-pearl buttons like a row of peas all the way down the spine, lace choking up at the throat. Never materialized, the daughter I saved it for.

Champagne

The lady at Parisian dry cleaners, a bridal gown *spécialiste*, employed mortuary words to assure me that the *eternity keepsake* box in which my dress, propped up on cardboard breasts, was *vacuum-sealed* and came with a lifetime guarantee. Which lifetime, or whose? *The marriage, that's some-zing else*, she said. *Love is more than a late-night snack.* I don't wonder. My husband's not one for staying up—oldest son of a French-speaking farmer, he's awake before cows are.

Eggshell

Thin, we called these the blown-out years. Around this time, I went to a dead/undead Halloween costume party as my latest head cold—smeared red lipstick on the rims of my eyes, Vicks VapoRub behind my ears, pinned Kleenex ghosts around the neck of a long black Morticia maxi. For such plainly faked misery, I got a lot of real sympathy. It brought out a faint lime tenderness in the zombie men.

What they don't tell you about the long haul

Then late one afternoon   exhausted from trying to find agreement
     we just
     take an impromptu nap   and for hours we rant in our sleep

Childless   we argue   about the values
     toys taught us as kids   beside the point but

Lack of the tangible has become accusation   poof
          the length of all our married years   minus
          what we have to show for it

          for now   nothing is solid

                    unmooring us

This chill   cured only by proximity   snuggling
          slouching towards closeness

Awake   and all is stark again
          hard on the eyes   dimming our prospects
                    our senses

In this low-ceilinged rented room   under the welcome mats and
     subfloor
               countless secrets

                    harden   in us

Late Valentine

Babe. I don't mean to be mean.
Our hokey ark, our true tribe? Yeah.
No me, no you, loners no more, *our*.
But you are not noël, I am not hark.
You're kale to my lamb, I'm llama
to your leek, my bite, your bark,
we're like a yurt, leaky, but normal,
a home. I bathe in you, you breathe me.

Not art, maybe, but rhyme, meter,
we are an elaborate labyrinth on the Tiber,
a three-minute mile, a Limerick mini-tour.
But beauty, only beauty, and no nite? Abnormal.
Or out of our mouths, only the truth? No, honey.
Heartbreak, all heartbreak, all the time.

Desaturation is a mind of dark blue

Illness takes on the disguise of love.
   —Virginia Woolf

blue and my tinged fingertips   is an everyday chest cold
                                                            turning dire

is the nearly indigo   oxygen-free stratosphere
                    as air sacs swell   lungs inflame

                    a blank slate   a shadow crossing lips
hospital alarms   breath crowded out

a circus tent
              deflating

      Dark blue is a shade
            once so lovely on me

      Not as becoming   the robin's egg blue
                    No   *pick midnight*

      Mom called it my color
                    You can carry it off

      The more deeply saturated
      the more sophisticated   that's what

      I miss   her confidence *for* me

I can't make a fist

Too soon   I'm wheeled
                    outdoors   the ex-patient zone

assaulted
            by car exhaust   faint

metallic smell   of bottled oxygen
                           fogged cannulae   tethering me

to a metered supply of the stuff
                                I step gingerly   off the curb

where ancestral wariness
                     dogs me

because in California   as in Italy
          lands where my fathers died

beware the ground   it may split
                           where you stand

and I may have to concede
                     to widening   crevasses

No longer *Teflon* or *spry* or *artful dodger*
My store of finesse has decamped

                                Dark blue
                           is the slipperiest of chasms

is the hitch at the bottom of exhale
               so much to it   and I've lost the knack

     There's a grandfather I've never met   Italian
                     American

sweet land of liberty
     The Great War

          shipped him back
               to fight against his own

     Mustard gas is a weapon
     of persistent inflammation

And ever after, he rasps
through scarred airways

demands quiet
craves the old days before radio

and scolds my father   for wasting
his   ever-loving   breath

All beings have been your mother

a Buddhist teaching

Winston-scented and coffee-breathed, bags under her eyes, fatigued beyond the reach of Excedrin, four children in five years. This was my mother. An old seven, I got stomachaches over how she'd ever manage. I washed dishes. I made my bed. Out of clay, I put together miniature inedible meals. Peas and carrots. Drumsticks. But I didn't know sewing. I had to have a choir robe to be in second grade chorus. White, like angels' clothes. Long, to my ankles. Without a white angel robe with a bow at the neck, I'd flunk choir. The next day in front of the blackboard, a rack of official choir robes. Exiled to a hook on the back wall of the classroom, Mom's version fashioned from Dad's old shirt which looked like a homemade ghost. I'd gotten the facts wrong. She'd stayed up all night. It made her sick all the next day. It killed her fifty years later. What did I know? In high school, my debate partner Doug was my mother. On the sly, he taught me how to drive his Dad's car, caught heck when I almost rolled it, took the blame, made me believe I could someday be a good driver. On filthy streets cracked with cold, a lady lived on cardboard, retrieved broken lipsticks from trash cans, stabbed color on her cheeks. Hadn't she been my mother? Singing that lullaby when I pressed dollar bills into her hand? *Sleigh bells ringing in the snow.* From one of my lovers, I caught the infection that locked off my womb. From some other girl he'd caught it, and she, from some other guy. All those lovers were my mothers. In other lifetimes, I was theirs. This scout ant crossing my yellow kitchen counter, a search party of one, looks for sustenance. I was of her tribe. She made an angel robe for me once.

Towards an uneasy love for Ophelia

O, you scattered, fragmented wisp, you
shattered flower pot shard, you torch singer
with no sense of pitch, how much I have learned
at your expense, from plight to plight
your *Ay, my lord* and *I think nothing, my lord*
that load you choke down, that we are born
to be mastered, you pawed-over unlucky charm.

          Yet, what would I give
for a sure and certain place in the chain of being?
How easy for pigeons to curtsy. How safe,
fixed at the feet of oaks, among vines, beneath
a seraphim canopy, to coast above the work song
clack of shellfish and the livelong undertow.

          And how much I ache
for a faith like yours, its wobbly legs, its puppyness,
how soft to give everything over, every muscle,
every ghost, to the collapsing fugue, to sleep—
because anyway, we are all of us weak, crying
uncle, life is weakness, and in every ending, we all lose
the will and the victory is without stones
in your pockets, and the river is your answer.

          O, Ophelia,
you deliver me from believing in ceilings
from the sway of swinging from some chandelier
and hearing what you would say come out of my mouth.
Who could deny me my moment of frailty,
talk me down from what ledge, keep me
from keening about my own stage? To be
a bad joke in the making? For want
of what would I press on?

But, Ophelia, you disaster,
you take my breath away—from the stinging nettles
in your hair to the reeds in your teeth—
as you breech the last lock so placidly,
you darling damned.

Fifteen

The low light in this black and white photo
accentuates your darkness, long pride of thick

brown hair, falling heavy past your shoulders
a bull's-eye paisley that just cups your breasts

riding high, the dirty dare of your parted lips.
You are away at camp—Ames

but it could be Gomorrah
imagining the trouble you want to get into.

The mutiny you committed in a cornfield
to the backbeat of the Easter Battle

of the Bands, chucking your virginity
to the first taker, not the boyfriend, quick

with slapping his name over yours, no,
you gave it to danger, an eighteen-year-old tough

with tougher East German hooks in him.
Unclaimable as unchecked luggage,

determined to twist out of captivity—
think: goldfish transferred by spoon

over a sink, down the drain to the ocean—
because where had belonging ever gotten

any woman except more belonging:
a second class ticket to sheets turned down

just so, to muumuu-land and baby-talk city.
And here you are summer, yawning, powerful

and pre-ripened.   Where you're standing,
the contrasts become you.

Pacific Grove, California

Ladies Sketch Club on the Beach, 1890

To order light   dear sister
to wield a vest pocket clock

and boss around the day
is not considered women's work

yet   truly   I live on scrapes
of Prussian blue and Gamboge crimson

go through tubes and tubes
of bright lead white
                    the cruelest white

for foam and spray   an ocean
pinned down with my palette knife

I'm under a raucous spell of light
and the sea swelling in me

the dried colors   caked
under my fingernails
                all the proof

I need   let my smocks   neglected
yellow and gray
               I don't care

only let me wait out
for the golden hour

see how it polishes even a crude thing
like my sweat   to a flushed glamour

it's not order   cleanliness
not our father's god I serve

behold my sin

like beach tar   whiskered blackly
in sand   and burnt umber

Purgatoire, Nevada

No breeze sister dear

scrape one cake lye soap
into boiling water   turn my head

smoke drifts dust   what a desert
won't draw out of a body

once believed I'd see mama again

sort into piles   colors britches
rags monthlies
                  insides still tender

whites soak in bucking tub   set with salt
pour boiling from a height
                        through wood ash
through grime tar blood

scrub scrub   knuckles smart
fingers thorned   til I can't stand my own touch

        for once let a stain just be

fetch fresh kettle of water   fresh
save the sweat dripping off my face

        fresh got a mouth on me

fish out scalded whites   make do
in a pinch use a broomstick handle

rinse starch   bluing   pin sheets
out of sight hang rags
                  repeat after me child

make your bed in the morning
and the day starts
                    sorrow bleaches us

pour rinse water in flower beds
flowers know your worth

sing morning   sing weak from heat
the devil vanquished   and a clean white smock

Beside my self with

I'd killed off two, maybe three of my selves
stuffed them in the broom closet—
why not the crawl space I wonder. Closets are the first places they look.

What it felt like to kill I don't remember except
in the bathroom with the cracked skylight
the roaches when I turned on the lamp to pee, the ants on the one cup
I didn't rinse before bed.

~~~

Only merely slightly against live and let live, slightly
Buddhist fraud.

On the lam, I'm invisible in mirrored Ray-Bans

when the noir version
where even the camera wields a scalpel
framed for something you didn't do
lights up my smart phone like a conscience, see?

~~~

Run into the actress playing me. Try to avoid her.
End up complimenting extravagantly.
She's so self-possessed. Knows about murders.
Her unruffled hippie chic, and underneath the floaty ruse—harsh as
    shitkicker boots.
Much better at this scene. More than one of me thinks, *Honey, you can
    have the part.*

~~~

Hole up in Manhattan. Try to blend in. Which who lives in this cold
    water flat?
Up a steep and very sorrid staircase. Interior decorated in paisley
    squalor.

Didn't Didi turn me on to this hide out?

I play shell-shocked, as happens in times like these
when words don't—spit it out . . . work.
Plus I've never been good with faces.

When I was who, what did I didn't do?
I must
belong here, don't I
keep coming back—I do. I do. Fuck. I do.
Eventually one feels assaulted by disguise.

Repertoire

The first impression I create is one of ugliness.

—Eleonora Duse
The Mystic in the Theatre

Westering

Dear soul,
> smudged collar of propriety
> darkened silver inheritance—

> I walk over fresh graves
> to join the headstrong winds,
> pushing past remnants

> of other outposts. Call it progress.
> Or one last claim hauled up
> blind from a rosewood chest.

Dear departed east,
> stranglehold
> of bone-on-bone china

> socked-in frosted windows
> and stunted limbs
> on old-growth trees,

> if death is a short cold
> then heaven, at my back,
> will be closer

> and once this westering
> sets up in me, like a conestoga
> I yearn so, surge by surge,

> for the wide satin vastness.

Dear knee,
> bent on the trail of folly
> which will not end with me—

Fourteen

is a moody smoldering punk with just enough bellows to forge a constant orange glare. **It** was fall again, former season of elation, filled with new-pencil, blank-notebook glee. I **was** autumn-stoned on grape-y mimeograph ink, floors lemon-waxed to ice rinks, **evening** and the good ache of light fading early, games of Red Rover wrapped up by streetlight 'til **all** the Dirks, and Ellens, and the girl we called Cream Cone got sent over. Late **afternoon** biology dragging on 'til we deep-sixed the lesson plan by subterfuge. On substitutes, **it** worked diabolical. Walking home, boys nearby, we rolled up our uniforms' waistbands—**was** it a sin to have nice legs? How pathetic keeping us safe all the time. From heavy **snowing** or some lame tornado warning. Dinner table parents drilling us on needing vs. wanting **and** how real mature it was doing hard things like giving away our dog for its own good—**it** didn't feel all that great to fail them but with expectations overshooting outer space, I **was** acne-bound to crap out in spectacular fashion, to break away from their story for me, **going** night-riding on the backs of motorcycles, braless, with bad boys, without helmets just **to** get away with it in secret and them clueless as their own youthful vibrance turned to **snow**. Under their noses, I'd come in, my hair reeking of weed, that's how *do you Mr. Jones* in **the** dark they were. *Fuck this,* I'd whisper into my sleeve. Black sheep, taken. I'd be **blackbird** of the family, bye bye. Twenty-four Octobers later. My godbaby has a hole in her heart. I **sat** biting my cuticles in a room devised to absorb after-images of red: talcum blue, watery art **in** Kleenex frames, décor by novocaine, a buffer zone to mute news that made my ears ring, **the** insanely measured tones of medicine men, always some crash cart in the hallways of **Cedar**-Sinai: slow up, careful, death hovers here, gravity forcing its lessons into my untested **limbs**.

Non Grata

We lay in the dark, breathing together.
—Louise Glück, *Faithful and Virtuous Night*

An indigo North Dakota winter night,
enter a girl, in between abandoned and thorn,
dirty blonde ribbon in her hair, B.O., annoyed,
an ongoing annihilation with knit brow. No hello.
Not likeable. Obliged to hear her rant, I try
to talk to the dear darkling. Nothing doing.
Oh, wow, tell me to go lie down and all day like garbage I rot.
A kid. Wary, daring, wayward. A tyrant.

By God, to be like that, a tangible knell,
world-weary energy all day, a lethal will
to hit the terrible wall again, letting go
like a battered door in wind. Her wronged tale,
hardly grand, we're nothing alike, are we?
Yet I let her go on. Let her reign the night.

Falling, failing like that

push off the high board, shove off the landing, down the elevator shaft, that same jolt when a foot doesn't account for a sudden valley, the sinking feeling in the stomach's pit just beyond the roller coaster's crest, descent into that shifty stretch of quicksand, gleaming slick of La Brea tar, blackout as in shooting to death's door, the grammar of danger in the color of ice, frozen clear, frozen cloudy, frozen milky green, frozen blue as in breaking through and slipping under, as in swimming farther out than heart can carry you back, as in curtains, done for, the thrash of ending, the look in your eyes the last time I saw your eyes, this widening, absence of upsway, sinking, falling, failing all along, what was that look, last look entrusted to me like a secret, is that this, this pull, this dire force, as if dragging you, your hands gripping me like a doorjamb, as if a stronger me could wrench you back.

World Gift Convention

In their artificial roses, Mom was a big seller, *in the top tier.*
She filled our fridge with chilled velvet bouquets, *Cold makes them curlier.*

For the July convention, she sewed a carnation-pink suit to wear.
It was her first creation *not a baby,* made of wash-and-wear wonder

fabric—Dacron double-knit, the latest thing.
She sewed for days, zigzag stitched through her pinky,

put her hand in her hair to keep blood off the jacket. *People think
redheads can't wear pink, but you have to choose the right pink.*

At the Dallas convention, among peers, she would know glory.
The welcome-home marigolds we picked, she placed on top of her
        gloves,

atop her handmade suit, laid where—shut up in Dad's trunk—it
        festered
all through summer, burnt the skirt orange. *Why can't I ever*

have nice things? Red-eyed, she banished her Very Easy Very Vogue
suit to the rag pile when mercifully that November, the rage

for that particular shade of pink abruptly died.

This June, Fireflies Carom Off the Glass Walls of Their Hotel Jars

Her skin, more windowpane than hide.
Her pulse, a moth trapped under tissue.

I spoon feed her
lemon slush
   glad for the chance
   to sit across from her
   on the bed

that great chenille country
from which she runs the other rooms.

Next door, summer's begun, loose
voices freed up with alcohol.

In this dim room, the heat's up so high
both of us have fevers.

I feel like a Tom Collins highball, she laughs,
ice cold and sweating. Her inhaler,

casual as a cigarette balanced between fingers,
chapped mouth, poised, open,

watery eyes, dilated and party jazzed.

Memory Foam

1.

Without a toxic berm
of chalky Ajax cleanser

to blockade the path
our ants would   go on

by rote   in single files
they would make

tiny time down
the scuffed wood

cabinet   the hinge
across a sandy foam

bathmat   and quiet
as a hairline crack

they'd perforate
the bright porcelain stage

of bathtub
a location

where one can
only get so clean

so washed of night.

2.

Powdered cleanser coats
their mandibles

abrasively
homes in   the way

a strong magnet
wipes out hard drives

they lose memory
lose their north

and south
retracing antic steps

from ledge to ledge.

3.

That's not all.
Now   termites too

eating   every
last   room.

To murder them
outright

with Foaming Bubbles
with Mercy Orange Oil

seems less cruel.
Some choices.

When you get older
you start to follow . . .

apart

4.

Dad   It's me
I'm your daughter

5.

Our new IKEA
memory foam bed

arrives the same day
as Dad's diagnosis

as our sleep
improves

as promises kept
with our restless legs

quelled   the separate
story problems of our bodies

imprinted
like cuneiform in clay

from way way off
over the din of insects

phones ring
and in darkness

new days begin
and because clocks

don't *transmit*
in his new tongue

Honey   Dad has to ask
what time is it?

and here   he sounds
unforgettably young.

Catch off the Venice Pier

Man reels in his catch—
a toy-sized leopard shark pup,
spotted and writhing,
maybe two pounds.

Man elbows
woman next to him
to drag their boy over.
Orders him to hoist
the struggling blur.
          Look at the phone, not the fish.
Woman's cell snaps.

Man lays his catch
on its belly, steps on its spine.
          That's only cartilage,
and unhooks the jagged lure, ripping
the baby-toothed shark
a new mouth.

Sets up the gasping carcass
for the next shot
and in a crimson spray, sinks it
back into the ocean, splash.

Boy curls his tongue under,
his eyes fastened on the escape route.

Taken to the Soil

In late September, the ground he picked out
warm yet, the boy lay down. His human days,
over, he had taken, quite devoutly,

to the soil.   Fall was heavy, drifts of rust
ballast for the voyage. He felt the knot
in his stomach un-sprool, become tap

root, his spine dowse for loam. He let
his lungs fill with spores, dust, the cast-off wings
of insects. He matched his breath to the suck

of the wind as glint ebbed to thrum, then hush,
he let the earth hear him out.
                                        Each day,

before school, his sister fills a bottle
from the tap, carries it to him by the neck.
Evenings, she scatters coffee grounds

flecked with gleaming eggshells, and quietly,
she stretches out next to him, their faces
                                        close as crossing lights.

This kindness written in rain

for Brigit Pegeen Kelly

In a humid trance, toward an open-air stage,
I trudge, a gangrenous mountain sky like a heavy
breather behind me in line. Under a cantilevered

eave stands Brigit, majestic as the cypress,
her gray-green eyes, the weather's mirror.
Last night, she keened *a low song a lost boy sings*

a wall of notes so honeyed, a strain so round
to the ear that I added a gasp at the swell.
Formal, in earth-colored habit,

she's a chalk turtleneck, shoes a shade of clay.
I'm a polka-dot mini-dress in an Amish church.
I resist feeling puny, flip, transient.

If only I had the gift for simple things.
If I had tall impossibles in store.
If I gave up small-time, would sacred follow?

Devotion to doubt's a drag. *Hell?*
It's so close you can walk there would be
something I'd write. Overhead, a deeper grumble

full of heckle and chuff, and breaking over us
like a fresh start, in comes a storm
that cuts in line, grabs the mic, pours.

Dear Modern Plastics Magazine,

Very heavy—

with your thick-stroke type, brash boldface lead-ins,
two-deck heads

your 22-lb. tree-hewn paper, fed to platen

stabbed in place by bail roller, pounced on
by steel letters fanned out in an iron orchestra pit

each by each, the line, the page, the slug

the nickel-plated spool snapping a red-up/black-down ribbon
like two-toned spectator shoes tracking dirt onto snow

carbon paper and the dinosaurs who died for it

sandwiched between triplet onionskin,
a crinkly harmony, bygone sisters

song, the silver bell each time the carriage reached lane's end

oily smells, definitive punctured stomps
of glossy progress and modern magazines,

crammed into steel files, filling a medium skyscraper

to the clouds—silly mortar, bricks and beams—
we're such lightweights, we, in the unimagined future

                    reading off thin air.

End over End: Endeavour

It was dumb luck.
I did not move a muscle

to stand with throngs
waiting for her to streak

over Griffith Park Observatory.
I did not tool down

to Santa Monica beach.
When KNBC threw it

to Colleen Williams,

> *She's just leaving Venice pier*
> *flying inland due east,*
> > *low and salutary,*

I was taking three steps out
onto an empty Culver street.

Boom. I, alone looked up to see you,
Endeavour—you death-defying sky queen

piggyback on a 747—fly over, dip,
and bank away, paying out a sonic wave

of shadow between us.

~~~

Dear Mom,

Imagine both you and Endeavour
in low houses now, hangared,

through with rising.
Again and again

it was dumb pain
and you wanting only to leave

> *Take me please*
> *away from here*

and Endeavour could only streak: bye-bye,
and I could only walk you to the gate.

I did not get your high cheekbones
from some Cherokee blood way back

or feel four souls come through me
or ever feel as inconsolable.

Lament nothing is how you lived
because nothing is ever really lost

but fearful of so much, not just oblivion—
the water, food, left turns.

It terrifies me how alive I feel, Mom.
To live on alone, to look up

and not see you with your head bent
toward a book, keeping your place

with chubby fingers, the same fatties
which type this note.

A failure of imagination
has cast us in different worlds.

I could fail you more by lamenting.
It is not such a leap to believe

you too can defeat gravity, Mom,
catch the mighty updraft

come out on high, a queen
and breaking with mere atmosphere,

in death, defy the percentages!
        You and Endeavour,

the hurtling acrobats, cross a pacific sky
become salutary shadows

        going wide and far from me.

Afterlife on Mars

When you died   out of obedience   before the climates could accord
Mars beckoned with scarlet arms.
You just turned something-nine   asleep on the hay and the dirt
    white field of worms.
Waterfalls gushed under wet skies.
And who'd've thought   solace could burn so   behind eyes sewn
    shut?

Meanwhile   outer space had exhausted   the patience of oxygen.
Stillness   keeps   a   hypnotizing   clock.
Earth, crossing signals   mixed up narrow minds   with wide open
    spaces.
No matter   you can eternally relive   every what moment.
Like a beach extinguishing itself   in blue.

You aren't a dragon slayer anymore.
The welcoming roundness   of red rocks—   you have it all on Mars.
And while your children misfire back here   you'll be gone.
But your past's ongoing   unlike the mouse in the field.
Out of this world   nothing   not even granite   decomposes.

The Geometry of Watching

Plant your feet in the night.
Hands in your pockets.

Triangulate those elbows.

Tense up the hypotenuse of each arm.
Finger on the trigger of a gun in every pocket.

Misters One, Two, Three and Four: stand in front
halfway between a huddle and a posse
        a pie slice away
        from parallel.

        And one of you,
        Mister Five,
        can lag behind.
                    Just that space
and we'll know you're suspicious.

Out of frame,
the light source is set to stun you
full in the face

        as the horizon cuts you off at the knees.

It's working now, guys.
Look at the light directly.
Give us your longest shadows.

Soliloquy

. . . first / violent love then
sweetness . . . First Norma
then maybe the Lights will play

—Louise Glück,
"Heart's Desire"

Start Talking

A girl comes
with her own light, shiny
as a gold anklet, milky
as a tan line, with platinum
capital she means
to spend, but don't look too hard
at those seams she's drawn
up her calves, or the pock marks
under that painted face.
So, she finds herself
a little man, a little rum,
a shot of honeysuckle, a LaSalle
to cross the tracks, beneath
the plunged neckline, check,
she's no nurse
and that perfect coiffure's not
her hair—it's a wig.
Loses all her teeth
the hard way, too, no smile,
no job at the checkout,
gets more employment
lying flat on the counter,
but she isn't the tuna hot
dish type and the scramble
to survive's not about eggs.
Pour her into a rocks glass
of pink wine, flame her
Lucky Strike, call her names,
she's rotten down to the bedrock,
honey, as fragrant as pigeon pie
as she slips a mickey in the monkey's
ice tea, gives him indigestion,
brings him to his knees,
railing straight down the line

isn't it rich he'd be the one
she'd go soft over?

Fifty

Supra Ventricular Tachycardia.
My racing heart, I'm a mustang

forced into a two-by-four stall,
an unshakeable oldest soul,

shaking. I choose a woman
cardiologist because I can't bear

to hear from a man
that I have to slow down,

give up the tight rope, the tryst,
the all-the-way living,

forsake the chase, stop pounding
the white and the black keys.

Because I've lied my whole life
like I thought a man would

beating first light out of bed,
out the door, leaving sex sweetly

snoring. Because my heart will fly
out of my chest, goldfish heart

slapping the counter to the beat
of an ear-bleeding Stratocaster

and the hammering pace
short circuits release, down

to the quick, this knife's edge.
Lookit, who's left to impress

anyway with my danger? Fast girl
bound to the little killer inside me.

Self-Defense Class

First, gouge his eyes out,
says a girl with a fearsome
amount of metal in her mouth,
and you think about what that first eyeball
will feel like under your thumb
as you keep going
even as the pressure changes.

Break his nose, says the girl with a head cold,
pound it with the heel of your hand,
like a ketchup bottle.

Rip his lip open, says tiny Rosemary.
Hook your fingernail in the corner
of his mouth and yank down hard.

A cruel second wind snaps through you—
cornflake-fed girls, meaned up on milk—
as you pair off for the finals
armed with dorm keys snug in the cleavage
above your knuckles, one keyed-up girl
for one attacker

the guys taking the class for their own reasons.
Helmeted, visored, cocooned in sleeping bags,
they waddle around the gym doing chubby dances
behind the teacher's back.

        Hurt him first, she says,
and it's like this—you whale on them, all of you
up on your tiptoes, you rage,
and it sounds like Nerf-ball hail,
and the guys smirk *cuz it tickles,*
and teacher's shiny brass whistle bounces
up and down off her trampoline-tight breasts—

it catches a shaft of light, it winks around,
it disco-balls the gym.

You practice self-defense in the momentary absence of peril.
You are red in the face. Ardently, you beat at air.

Arachne's Lament

She ubers home, somber
from yet another memorial

but the driver wants
leetle kiss like bee-sting. No charge.

Was a time
she could trap, trick and suck

the life out of him. No more.
Take me to the danker side,

she mouths drowsily. Dropped off
at her stop, she watches the bug

gain traction on the gravel
pummeling her with jagged things—

comes the laugh track of the street
a *honk honk* and a frog croak

and other moonless abscesses.
Once, she wore the garment,

not the other way around.
Now, absent-mindedly

she catches her silk mesh on a nail.
Hello cobwebs, she hails her hovel.

She makes the best of it
like other black widows do—

but it's loveless
settling for a defanged life,

speaking in a small voice,
mending gowns with spittle.

She Doesn't Love You

Imagine her, happy, sitting in your passenger seat,
the unwritten you at the story's wheel, all Brut aftershave

and chrome-shiny you, driving the buttermilk-yellow Camaro

out of Omaha, brand new, leather buffed back to beef.
On this midwestern June night, the fecund

perfume of skunk, corn floss, manure turned loam

streaming through rolled down windows,
you say, *I'm going places,* and this time, she believes you.

And at the long stoplight,

you kiss her the way you always meant to,
parting her chapel veil of Heaven Scent, soft

on the shut cherry of her mouth, you coax it open

and can still taste—will chase through time
the whole wide fragrant future—

and ahead, the road, straight as facts.

Strangled, Eventually

Murder works up an appetite.
Strangled, no less—those kitten kicks,
the faked tussle for the car door.
A girl gets banged around for real,
all that pretend terror.   A night shoot,

Pearblossom Highway, factor
in the desert—3AM's nothing
like 3PM.   She's not dressed,
she's draped in a low-cut handkerchief
they call a costume, just two swipes

of Love That Red
to keep her lips from turning blue.
So cold, her gasps send up smoke
signals in the key light, not a wrap
in sight, no one to rescue her save

this miscast pretty-boy killer.
It's in the script—she croaks.
But he's so green, he giggles,
Sorry, take after muffed take,
cracks his knuckles, giggles more.

Please kill me, she whimpers,
teeth chattering next to his ear.
You're trembling, he purrs.
She snarls, *I am starving you doofus.*
Fuck wispy.

The House Goes to Half

The theatre is a place to which one goes
less in the hope of complete illusion
than in the hope of being only half-way disillusioned.
　　—George Jean Nathan, "The Popular Theatre" (1918)

At *places* for the Sunday matinee, top of Act Two, the actress suffers.
　　　　Her sweaty wig itches something terrible.
　　The exit signs abruptly extinguish, the huge room
closes in as if by massive descending cloak.

Little squeals erupt, trilled off steam of expectation—
　　　　the audience wants a carpet ride or at least a small bonfire.
　　In the wings, behind the drapes they call tormentors, she waits.
She'll make the same down left cross from last night (18 hours ago)

and from the matinee (6 before that) facing the matte side
　　　　of the flimsy night scrim, the peeling stick-um
　　rhine-stars above her, the blue-gelled backstage air tense,
that certain end-of-the-week tang wafting off Elizabethan costumes.

And then in a self-willed trance, the character's lofty thoughts
　　　　commence to crowd out her petty cares again.
　　To the thousand pinches submit,
and what scabs for art she's obliged to pick

eight shows a week. On the hook for a two hour life,
　　　　borrowed off the balance of her own,
　　the words, committed to mind, fine-combed over for nuance,
raveled, unraveled, rehearsed to sound composed

on the spot. Pauses an eye bat long, pauses
　　　　all the King's horses could ride through.
　　Her seasoned body, an instrument of verse, channel
for the precise note stranded in a long-suppressed *Oh* . . .

and beneath sound, the felted silence, a stealth text, the prickly
            underpinning for the whine of her character's charge:
    . . . and I have borne, and borne, and borne and have been fubbed off,
and fubbed off, and fubbed off from this day to that day . . .

all of it said, never said, said never before this way.
            And again, she will enter, all decked out.
        The follow-spot sun will dog
her every step, racking hot on the rising and falling

of her lilac powder-puffed chest.
            The lekolite will widen like a dilated pupil.
        The fresnels will go full tilt.
The combustion of all that pyrotechnic attention. Wow.

For this one moment of the day,
            (twice on Saturdays and Sundays)
        her rounded ruddy face is a vision
from which it will be impossible to look away.

In her period corset, tight, vise tight,
            her voice strains, she's running out of air—
        so she will *use* it, this breathlessness
to sound whispery and coarse. Her pleasance . . . on edge!

Effortlessness is ninety-nine percent perspiration.
            All so that a lone woman's plaintive voice
        may insist, to these listeners, playing out
past the rafters, and beyond this little room's sweet spot.

Our Lady of Desires

. . . the creative act is not performed by the artist alone . . .
—Marcel Duchamp

He lays her blank body down
while it's being assembled
        supple as a late afternoon

        open for creation
his touch inventing her
his hands father
        her every curve

        then carefully wrapping
he puts her away
        where she will crack.

        For years, he fixes her
closes her tears
        layer upon layer fashions her

           expressionless, suspended
           like a swollen plum in garnet syrup,
           half hidden from him, especially him.

He stares, stares at her,
        cherishes her,
           stared at.

        From a great height falls

              a river
        cutting loose a rushing grace

the fading light ripens
        the very moment
        fruit splits. . .

let the dusk clothe her

now detach with abandon

oh nice touch, the gas lamp

his his his his his   will sing.

Anniversary of a Crime

Every year, the same gift—he calls me when rates get cheap,
wakes me after three, keeps me on the line for hours burning it up,
smoking like a mobster, until he's parched white noise.
>   *No one hears anymore. Deaf people*
>   *all over the place.*

Gone, I'll bet, that cashmere suit of his, the color of snow
in a summer weight, brash as gold flapping on a clothesline,
so of course, I fell for it, let him bury his face in my strawberry hair,
threw all my cards in with his, the pair of us, honeyed and uncontrite—
what a confection of criminals we made.

Just that now, with dawn coming on so tarnished,
when he says, exhale turning to static,
>   *Sometimes night's the only shoulder I got left to cry on,*
Jesus, he's hard to take.

Down and Allow

I hadn't washed my hair that morning   because   I'd planned on
doing it after, was running   late all day   (and then all of a sudden,
time didn't matter).   Was wearing shorts, had gone on an errand in
the Valley   thighs stuck to the seat   had no jacket, had the wrong
clothes on and I think I slept in them that night, I must have.   I'd
gotten on the highway and just flown by my exit   when all I wanted
was the day to roll backwards.

You know he never seems   enthusiastic   over my endeavors, yet the
minute   I   let down and allow   any of my own   feelings to show
other than enthusiasm that is, he gets depressed.

I saw another young girl   passed out on the sidewalk. I was drinking
cold coffee   and she was splayed ear to the ground, head towards the
crosswalk   as if listening for the light to change.   The next thing   I
wanted to happen however unlikely   I wanted to be abducted by
aliens, again   different aliens.   *Come Take Me*, I said to the air.

The Circe Effect

Oh let's just be hogs, cried an old hog.
           —Russell Edson, "A Performance at Hog Theatre"

The rude bristle
of his unshaven face

sprouting rough
against your cheek—sick,

this Duroc
at the mixer,

all squinty beams
and truffle breath,

barging into choleric rants
scoffing at infection

and you, anemic,
break into a rash—

splotched and earthy,
your jittery laughter.

And with a little cough,
you squat astride him

in an intimate sty,
oinked up

for porky snorts and squealing
and crying too hard

that screamy sound—
half rapture (torture!)—

you, spanked with paprika
you, a sneezing choo-choo

slicking up every inch
of a balled-up toilet paper wad—

can't get his carnal contagion
out of your system—

wrecked, wracked and reeking
you, so effulgently swine.

Double Cross

The wind will rat you out
like a rotary dial racking back

like footsteps on the floor overhead
grinding grit into a hardwood knot.

Your shiny-eyed confidence comes on
like distraction, a loud blaze of checkered

past—jacket, tie & plastered on,
man oh man, that combustible smile.

So what's a foolproof plan worth?
Who says there's no glory in comeuppance?

It's little you against expensive suits,
glass-paned cages, steep staircases,

suspension bridges, streets slicked down
with dusk.   That squalid stretch of river, late.

Get a clue. Do nothing. Walk away. Wake up.
The next sure thing's barbiturate—

the more you bag, the calmer your nerve:
you're a small-timer itching for big,

spending large on one last take,
one eye out for the back back-way

cuz every low slung slipper club
might be the next Venus fly trap—

it's in the furry air, babe,
tonight, tomorrow night or any night—

listen to the band play
"Twilight Time,"

catch how casually
the guy, sounds like Judas,

drops your name.

The blind know about daydreams

Darla, this make-up artist I worked with,
had had some horrible
crack-up, got her face Frankenstein'd back on
sideways with staples—she looked pieced together mid-seizure.
So, Darla startled the stars, well,
everyone, at first,
though a self-deprecating way
can go far in Hollywood,

surprisingly.   *O I don't mind the stares, she liked to joke.*
Being shunned is worse.
She had to begin long before dawn, laboring over *her* face,
rutted scarlet running welts, ruby grafts and rilled edges
pinked into her forehead.
She slathered on her Joe Blasco #1 concealer—
Yellow distracts red.
Then she'd strap a see-thru sling of mortician-made Illusion
to her shattered-in-nine-places chin.
Two hairpieces—a Polynesian fall, and a fringe that just grazed

her lashless lids.
One time,
this actor (some ruthless killer type)
stepped up into the makeup trailer she kept meat-locker cold,
got a load of Darla and gasped in a high squeak,
rubbed his face, gruff,
and within an instant, all was out-wattaged
by his flashbulb smile.
In the picture business
love is just a re-take away.

It's an honor to work in movies, she told the make-believe killer,
attending to the beautiful, she didn't stop,
rigging perfect faces for the camera's x-ray gaze,

it's a gas to match skin shades to names:
you're Dior Suntan, I'm Cinema Secret Champagne, each face,
another stray to lay hands on,
she said through Invisaligned

teeth, *then you're mine on the day.*
She was serious. She really put her back into it,
wielded the finest grade sandpaper, buffed off
the trails of capillaries,
tiny crap the high-def sees,
played up his facial symmetry—
left side, right side, identical.
It looks more demonic
all the while her face close enough and in position

to kiss.
She talked to her actors in the looking glass,
fake face to fake face (the way we picture-types conversed)
applying disguise after disguise
and on display, reflected in mirrors that ran the length of the trailer—
all day Darla
known for her gentle, scathing, unscathed hands.

Of matchbooks, phone booths and the loss of Nickodells

In those days, when somebody famous
        yanked open the bar's side door off Melrose,
spilling a rectangle of sunny rebuke
            on us unknowns ripening
in Nickodells's night-for-day ambience,
        we looked up without looking up
slitting our eyes to the light.
            We were dark-clothed theater rats
rehearsing all hours in our black box empty spaces
        on our wage-less farce, our German Expressionism,
all our daylight eaten, not-from-around-here-pale,
            funhouse sweaty with thirst to burn.
But seated in a place like Nickodells
        in old Hollywood, on the slightly seedy side
down from local television station K-Cal
            and spooned by the back lot of Paramount Studios,
in the hierarchy of regulars, we had rank.
        We wanted for nothing.
Nickodells, with a name like loose change,
            where dream makers on martini lunches
and newscasters—*from the desert to the sea*
        to all of Southern California—like Jerry Dunphy,
could tuck into one of the bar's red leather booths
            and dine in the cocktail atmosphere,
where good old nobodies
        could have a completely appointed experience,
exchanging numbers inside midnight blue matchbooks
            that boasted of air-conditioning,
a smoky topaz back-mirrored bar,
        Caesar salads tossed tableside,
shoestring potatoes salty hot,
            dark wood, dark corners, fifteen different bourbons—

back when drinking in the daytime
           was the mark of a vivid lush life,
when you could pick up matchbooks
       by the handful, next to the cigarette machine
on the way to the phone booth
          acting like you had somebody who loved you
dying for a call.

Went for a swim in the ocean at night, only I don't and

Bette Davis is teaching us camera angles,
then I walk home from the Haight, which is far
without a lens. She takes the measuring tape—
the kitchen wall's covered with fruit pulp,
the camera sits on a tarp of crushed Life Savers,
the breakfast nook's set up like a sick bed—
and wraps around all three of us (who's third?) (who's sick?)—
the living room just goes on and on, must be fifteen couches;
and it's a yard to her nose. She starts braying, *Wipe my mouth.*
Customers line up, waiters sweep in with huge handkerchiefs,
jacarandas growing wild over tables, you should've seen her
up close, dream close, like breathing in a purple knock-out mask.

Nameless In Paris

Off the steel lace of Eiffel
I launch myself
and it's just a matter of angle, this flying,

levitating really, without strain
and next to me on the night he's died,
Marlon Brando flies too,

right through French doors,
cups his hand over my mouth,
his face within my bite

No names here. Not . . . one . . . name—
Brando
when beautiful

was a weary thug. I'm dreaming
in cinema, again, which is all I know
of Paris and I'm sick to death

of gravity, the ache I feel
where wings should be. I want
to slough off the places

where I'm known,
the many rooms of my renown,
summer picnics where I lugged

a heavy coat, dipped not one toe
in the water and woke up tethered
to a map. Never lost my way going home.

Let me slip back into a bathwater night
in this city of flight. Let my body pour out easy
following the river I've heard

runs through Paris. Weightless.
Aloft. Anonymous at last
among the French stars.

Part of a Lifetime

Mom needs potassium. *Bananas,* I say,
then her line, *It's twue,* and there we are again,

in a vaudeville routine. She smells like a perfume
that's gone off, and her timing's

shot. *I did a heart attack on Seventh Heaven. Wanna see?*
Take it easy, drawls the intake nurse.

In the morning, she phones Dad on her hospital orange-juice can,
Honey, good news—overnight, I learned Japanese!

Doctor Snows prescribes Dilantin, stat,
the tall world, flat, that's what Mom needs.

By the matinee, she's down to two words:
Another   Coincidence.

The next day,
she's a silent movie.

On the third day of her hospital engagement, like champagne
      uncorked,
Mom talks for fourteen hours, no intermission, speaking on the inhale

to hold the floor, her clattering hands, *I've always wanted to be ambivalent*
she crows, careening in grand loop-de-loops of tirade—

she is Lucky, WAITING FOR GODOT, *Qua Qua Qua,* and all day
as the meal trays pile up, and the sun changes shifts with the moon,

I watch her scale this huge monologue,
the biggest part she's ever had, persevering

even after she's lost her audience, all
save me, standing by, I know,

to go on for her.

Eclipse: A Midday Gloaming

What we see, we see
and seeing is changing
        —Adrienne Rich, *Planetarium*

Through a pinhole in writing paper
a tiny crescent of sunshine wobbles

on white cardboard. It mesmerizes
our neighbors from Hyderabad.

In broken English, they thank us,
bowing in the fleeting dusk,

pressing their palms into steeples.
In Bavaria, Emperor Louis,

believing he was seeing the event horizon
for his flat 9th-century world, died of fright

in the darkened doorway where he stood.
There's no shortage of phenomena

on which to wish total eclipse
yet the universe, a Möbius strip,

is inexorably mad for cycles
and not accepting, again we ask:

Now what.
We'll make the same mistakes.

Issue apologies. Vow to love
better and soon renege because

some days
are wonderless?

This morning turned twilight
and on cue, a blackbird

flew nightward to her nest,
and rose at second daybreak

loyal to the rhythms of her one life:
light, dark, light, dark, light.

Notes

"A Doll's House" was inspired by the Mabou Mines production of the Ibsen play in which all the men were played by actors under four and a half feet in height and all the women were over 6 feet tall.

"Summer Calling" is meant to evoke John O'Keefe's Padua Hills Playwrights Festival production of his play, "Bercilak's Dream," an out of doors, in an open field, beckoning the day to end performance at sunset.

"Late Valentine" is oulipo-esque in that its vocabulary derives from a phrase in Carl Phillips' poem "Radiance versus Ordinary Light" . . . *I'll break your heart, break mine.*

"Westering" was a term used for heading out for the great western frontier in Joan Didion's "Where I Was From." Additionally, I took as inspiration this passage: ". . . each arriving traveler had been reborn in the wilderness . . . the very decision to set forth on the journey had been a kind of death, involving the total abandonment of all previous life."

"Fourteen" began as a golden shovel poem (thank you Terrance Hayes), each line ending in the words, in sequence, of the last stanza of Wallace Steven's "Thirteen Ways of Looking at a Blackbird." It has become a variation. Now, it's an Easter egg golden shovel poem with the original end words in bold, in sequence, "hidden" inside the body of the poem.

"Non Grata" is also oulipo-esque; the vocabulary is from the Louise Glück epigraph.

"This kindness written in rain" quotes lines from both "Song," by Brigit Pegeen Kelly, to whom this poem is dedicated, and an earlier poem of mine, "Limbogodisappearo."

"Dear Modern Plastics Magazine," references the McGraw Hill publication, which in 70s Manhattan, before virtual cloud storage, had to be typed from front to back, generating an actual wall of IBM Selectric sound.

"Geometry of Watching" is an ekphrastic take on *Watching*, an oil painting by Goran Djurovic which hung at Obsolete, a Venice, California art gallery.

"Start Talking" imagines if Phyllis (Barbara Stanwyck) was the one telling the story in the *Double Indemnity* (1944) voiceover instead of Walter (Fred MacMurray).

"The House Goes to Half" quotes lines from Mistress Quickly in William Shakespeare's "Henry IV, Part Two."

"Our Lady of Desires" was Marcel Duchamps' pet name for his last piece of art, over which he labored for twenty years. Installed at the Philadelphia Museum of Art only after his death, and entitled *Ètant Donnes* (translation: Given: 1. The Waterfall 2. The Illuminating Gas). At twenty-one, I worked there and took my break in the corner of that room, watching people walk up to the old Spanish door, find the peep holes, and jump back.

"Double Cross" is inspired by Richard Widmark in the film, *Night and the City* (1950).

Acknowledgments

I am grateful to the editors of the following journals, online zines and anthologies in which these poems (sometimes in slightly different forms) first appeared. Thank you Larry Colker, Jim Doane, Alexis Rhone Fancher, Lisa Grove, Mifanwy Kaiser, Jeffrey Levine, Suzanne Lummis, Eric Morago, Jim Natal, Lorine Parks, Cathie Sandstrom, Susan Terris, Lynne Thompson, C.M. Tollefson, and Samantha L. Woods.

Apeiron Review: "This kindness written in rain"

California Journal of Poetics: "Non Grata"

Cathexis Northwest Press: "Standard Time," "Down and Allow," "Falling, failing like that," "Towards an uneasy love for Ophelia"

Cultural Weekly: "Of matchbooks, phone booths and the loss of Nickodells," "Counting Off-Whites on the Fingers of One Hand," "Late Valentine," "Pacific Grove, California / Ladies Sketch Club on the Beach, 1890," "Purgatoire, Nevada / Washday," "Beside my self with"

High Shelf: "What they don't tell you about the long haul"

In Posse Review: "Summer Calling," "Geometry of Watching"

The Malpais Review: "Anniversary of a Crime"

Tulane Review: "Westering"

Speechlessthemagazine: "Strangled, Eventually"

Spillway: "A Doll's House," "Dear Modern Plastics Magazine,"

Tupelo Quarterly: "Taken to the Soil"

Anthologies—
1001 Nights: "Non Grata"

Beyond The Lyric Moment: "The Circe Effect"

But Who's Counting: "Dear Modern Plastics Magazine,"

Dark Ink: A Poetry Anthology of Horror: "Correcting for death"

Poet's Calendar: "Taken to the Soil"

A Personal Note

To my husband and inspiration, Leon Martell, for his patience and unconditional love—*when you're near me, wonderful things come to be* (The Fantasticks). To my beloved late parents, Al Ruscio and Kate Williamson, who instilled in me a passion for reading and the sound of words in the air—our love has no end. For my brother Michael, sisters Maria and Nina, you are my built-in best friends, thank you for everything. To my large extended family: in-laws, cousins, nephews, nieces, grandnephews, grandnieces—heaping portions of love. To my "longest" friend, Vicki Skarin, whose honest opinion is worth the world to me. To Laurie O'Brien and Carl Weintraub who embrace every version of me. To Shannon Holt and our Cinema Club forever. To Lorinne Vozoff, my spiritual mother. A debt of gratitude to Dorothy Barresi and her manuscript reordering magic. A profound thank you to Keith Badowski and his Brick Road Poetry Press for choosing this book and collaborating on its making. Keith's counsel, patience and insight were invaluable. Always gracious, he's been a real prince to this poet. A shout out thank you to Ace Boggess for keeping me hyphen-correct. This book would also not exist without the many acts of encouragement, the uncountable hours spent together in workshops, and the grace and wisdom bestowed on me from the many teachers, mentors, fellow poets, first readers and colleagues—my poetry's been enriched by all of you. I will try (and fail, but try again) to name you all. First, the teachers and mentors: Stephanie Waxman, Laurel Ann Bogen, the late Philomene Long, Suzanne Lummis, Cecilia Woloch, David St. John, B.H. Fairchild, Ellen Bass, the late Brigit Pegeen Kelly, Dorianne Laux, Sarah Maclay, Gail Wronsky, Dorothy Barresi. Also first, my colleagues, fellow writers and poets: Carine Topal, Cathie Sandstrom, Jerry Garcia, Kathleen Lohr, Claudia Handler, Mark Beaver, Judith Pacht, Lynne Thompson, Candace Pearson, Brenda Yates, Mary Fitzpatrick, Kim Young, Keven Bellows, Susanna Styron, Lois P. Jones, Peggy Dobreer, Kate Hovey, Marjorie Becker, Cece Peri, Barbara Blatt, Hilda Weiss, Lisa Grove, Zachary Greenberg, David Eadington, Jessica Goodheart, Marilyn Robertson, Roger Soffer, Jim Natal, Jeannette Clough, Jan Wesley, Steve McDonald, Adele Slaughter, Alice Tuan, Amy Davis, Amy Schulz, Ann Bronston, Elizabeth Iannaci, Brendan

Constantine, Betzi Richardson, Bill Mohr, Frank Kearns, Patti Scruggs, Jacqueline Tchakalian, Brian Tracy, Michelle Bitting, Brighde Mullins, Darrell Larson, Elena Karina Byrne, Charlotte Innes, Merle Kessler, Dean Petrakis, Dodds Musser, Doug Knott, Beth Amato, Rick Lupert, Elaine Mintzer, Elena Secota Martell, Eric Vollmer, Greg Itzin, Hari Budgen, Jane Otto, Jean Holloway, Laurel Ollstein, Julie Hébert, Laural Meade, Chris Wells, The Secret City, John O'Keefe, John Steppling, Talia Shire Schwartzman, Beverly D'Angelo, Julie Marie Myatt, Lory Bedikian, Katherine Penney, Kathleen Lohr, Terry O'Quinn, Laurel Blossom, Maria Ruiz, Marlane Meyer, O-lan Jones, Michael Harris, Michael C. Ford, Murray Mednick, Guy Zimmerman, Nancy Munson, Oliver Mayer, Paul Lieber, Jeanne Field, John Binder, Susan Krebs, Rob Roberge, Roland "Vachine" Vassin, Roxanne Rogers, Sam Anderson, Sissy Boyd, Shawna Casey, Stephany Prodomides, Susan Ahdoot, Susan Hayden, Shannon Cochran, Michael Canavan. In memory and gratitude to Carroll Kearley, Terry Stevenson, Bruce Williams, Larry Colker, Robert Rigamonti and Erica Erdman. There is no end to the list of friends, new and old, far and wide, whom I hold dear and carry in my heart—you are *the unsayable sums, joyfully add yourself* (Rilke). This book is for all of you.

About the Author

Beth Ruscio, daughter of actors, is part of a working class family of artists, actors, teachers and writers working in California. Her poetry has been Pushcart Prize and Best of the Net nominated and won finalist honors for several prizes and awards: The Wilder Prize, The Sunken Garden Poetry Prize, The Tupelo Quarterly Prize, The Ruth Stone Poetry Award and The Two Sylvias Prize. She was the second prize winner in Beyond Baroque's Best Poem Contest, was named a Newer Poet by Los Angeles Poetry Festival and won the Patricia Bibby Scholarship to Idyllwild Poetry awarded by Cecilia Woloch. *Speaking Parts,* her first full-length collection, won the Brick Road Poetry Prize.

A featured poet and frequent contributor to *Cathexis Northwest Press*, as well as *Cultural Weekly*, other recent work has been published in *Tupelo Quarterly*, *Tulane Review*, *Spillway*, *Malpais Review*, *High Shelf*, and is forthcoming in *Apeiron Review*. Her poems also appear in the anthologies *Dark Ink: Poetry Inspired by Horror*; *Beyond the Lyric Moment*; *1001 Nights*; and *Conducting a Life: Maria Irene Fornes*.

Ruscio is also an accomplished, award-winning film, television and theatre actress, and a longtime mentor at Otis College of Art and Design. She shares her life with her husband, the gifted playwright and teacher Leon Martell and their talented dog Lolita.

Discover more: please visit her website at bethruscio.com.

Our Mission

The mission of Brick Road Poetry Press is to publish and promote poetry that entertains, amuses, edifies, and surprises a wide audience of appreciative readers. We are not qualified to judge who deserves to be published, so we concentrate on publishing what we enjoy. Our preference is for poetry geared toward dramatizing the human experience in language rich with sensory image and metaphor, recognizing that poetry can be, at one and the same time, both familiar as the perspiration of daily labor and as outrageous as a carnival sideshow.

Available from Brick Road Poetry Press

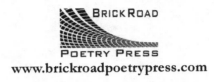

BRICK ROAD

POETRY PRESS

www.brickroadpoetrypress.com

The Word in Edgewise by Sean M. Conrey

Household Inventory by Connie Jordan Green

Practice by Richard M. Berlin

A Meal Like That by Albert Garcia

Cracker Sonnets by Amy Wright

Things Seen by Joseph Stanton

Battle Sleep by Shannon Tate Jonas

Lauren Bacall Shares a Limousine by Susan J. Erickson

Ambushing Water by Danielle Hanson

Having and Keeping by David Watts

Assisted Living by Erin Murphy

Credo by Steve McDonald

The Deer's Bandanna by David Oates

Creation Story by Steven Owen Shields

Touring the Shadow Factory by Gary Stein

American Mythology by Raphael Kosek

Waxing the Dents by Daniel Edward Moore

Also Available from Brick Road Poetry Press

www.brickroadpoetrypress.com

Dancing on the Rim by Clela Reed

Possible Crocodiles by Barry Marks

Pain Diary by Joseph D. Reich

Otherness by M. Ayodele Heath

Drunken Robins by David Oates

Damnatio Memoriae by Michael Meyerhofer

Lotus Buffet by Rupert Fike

The Melancholy MBA by Richard Donnelly

Two-Star General by Grey Held

Chosen by Toni Thomas

Etch and Blur by Jamie Thomas

Water-Rites by Ann E. Michael

Bad Behavior by Michael Steffen

Tracing the Lines by Susanna Lang

Rising to the Rim by Carol Tyx

Treading Water with God by Veronica Badowski

Rich Man's Son by Ron Self

Just Drive by Robert Cooperman

The Alp at the End of My Street by Gary Leising

About the Prize

The Brick Road Poetry Prize, established in 2010, is awarded annually for the best book-length poetry manuscript. Entries are accepted August 1st through November 1st. The winner receives $1000 and publication. For details on our preferences and the complete submission guidelines, please visit our website at www.brickroadpoetrypress.com.

Winners of the Brick Road Poetry Prize

2018

Speaking Parts by Beth Ruscio

2017

Touring the Shadow Factory by Gary Stein

2016

Assisted Living by Erin Murphy

2015

Lauren Bacall Shares a Limousine by Susan J. Erickson

2014

Battle Sleep by Shannon Tate Jonas

2013

Household Inventory by Connie Jordan Green

2012

The Alp at the End of My Street by Gary Leising

2011

Bad Behavior by Michael Steffen

2010

Damnatio Memoriae by Michael Meyerhofer